This Walker book belongs to:

To Grandad for sparking and nurturing my love of bees, gardening and agriculture when I was very young, and to The Beekeeper for re-igniting that same love, many years later. MD.

For Elana, our busy bee of flight. With love. MH

The Beehive
First published in 2024
by Walker Books Australia Pty Ltd
Gadigal and Wangal Country
Locked Bag 22, Newtown
NSW 2042 Australia
www.walkerbooks.com.au

This edition published in 2026

Walker Books Australia acknowledges the Traditional Owners of the country on which we work, the Gadigal and Wangal peoples of the Eora Nation, and recognises their continuing connection to the land, waters and culture. We pay our respect to their Elders past and present.

A catalogue record for this book is available from the National Library of Australia

ISBN: 978 1 761601 69 9

The illustrations for this book were created with watercolours on Arches paper
Typeset in Bembo Book MT and Oranges and Lemons
Printed and bound in China

EU Authorized Representative: HackettFlynn Ltd,
36 Cloch Choirneal, Balrothery, Co. Dublin, K32 C942, Ireland.
EU@walkerpublishinggroup.com

10 9 8 7 6 5 4 3 2 1

CREDITS

Thank you for your bee wisdom, research and knowledge…

- Len Arkadieff *'Lenny the Legend'* of Golden Ark Honey
- Murray Arkadieff *'The Beekeeper'* of Farmgate Honey
- Dr Toby Smith of Bee Aware Kids
- Tim Heard of Sugarbag Bees
- Annie Fanning and Tom Banks of St Aidan's Anglican Girls' School for bringing my Earth Angels schemes to life.

Megan Daley Max Hamilton

The BEEHIVE

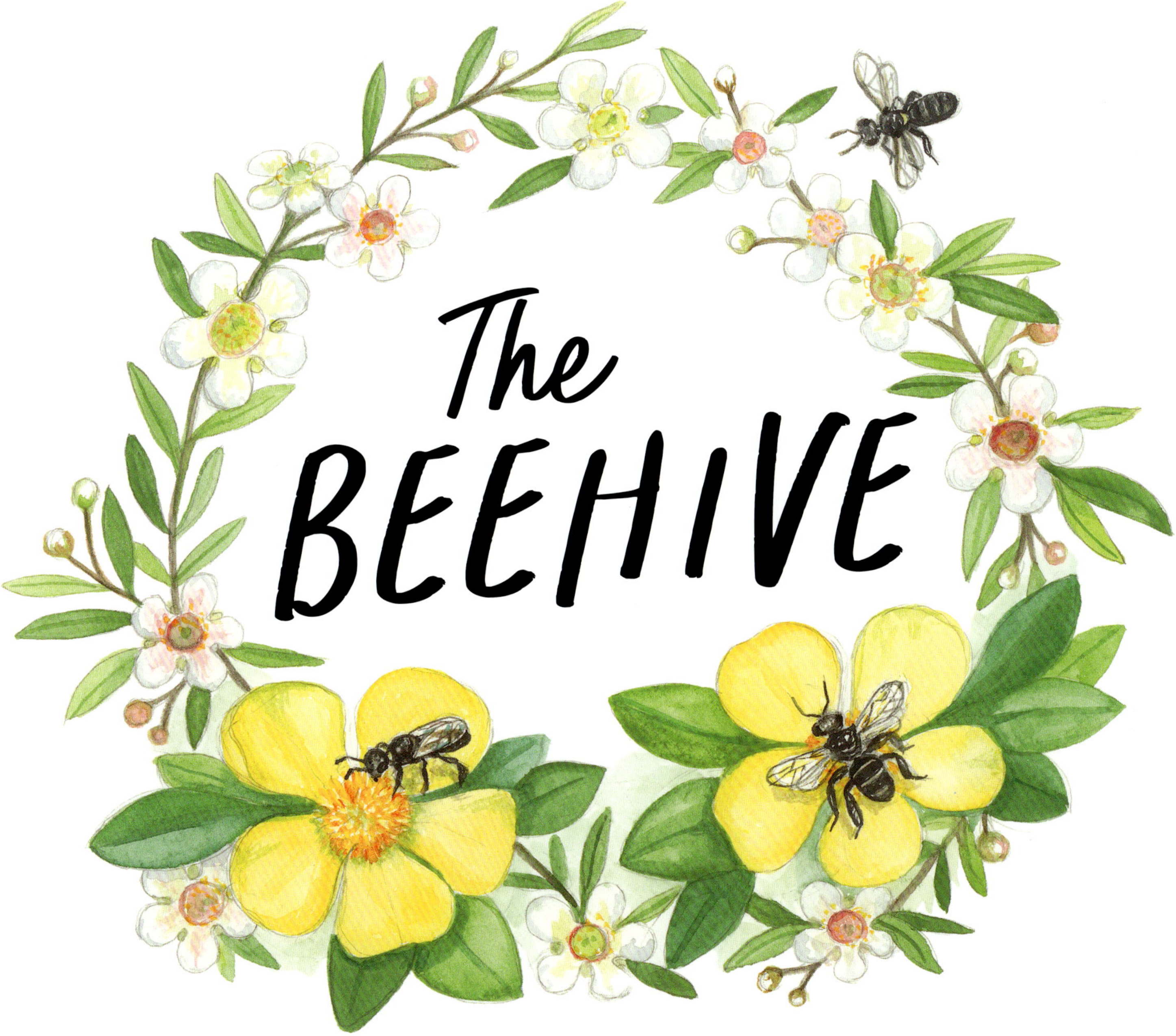

Each morning Willow hurried to school to spend a few moments alone with her most favourite creatures in the world, the native stingless bees.

Willow counted as the bees flittered on teeny grey wings towards the *hive* and crawled in through the opening. She cheered those who carried loads of *pollen* and she wished luck to each *foraging* bee.

Australia has around 2000 varieties of native bee species.

Some bees are solitary and nest alone, only coming together to mate, while others are semi-social, building nests close together.

Like the European honey bee, some Australian native stingless bees are highly social and live in a hive with one queen and thousands of workers.

EUROPEAN HONEY BEE

NATIVE STINGLESS BEE

Hive health can be inspected externally by looking at foraging activity and measuring the weight of the hive and observing its sounds and smells.

Groundskeeper Tom was in charge of inspecting and dividing the hives for the school's Nature Club.

Willow's favourite mornings were the ones when Tom would sit with her quietly and watch the bees toil away. Willow was yet to find a question he could not answer about native bees.

It was Tom who had first shown the children the native beehive in the hollow of an old tree and its build-up of *resin* near the entrance, a sure sign of bees about.

Willow wanted to capture the sharp, sweet aroma of the hive so she could smell it forever.

Native stingless bees generally use propolis to build their nests, as it sets hard and is waterproof. Propolis is a mix of beeswax and sticky resin collected from plants by forager bees.

Willow now noticed native bee nests everywhere!

With the school native bee numbers increasing, Willow and her family put themselves on the list to receive their own hive from the yearly divide. She had waited, not-very-patiently, for it to be their turn.

Native stingless bees are
sometimes mistaken for flies!
They will often make their
nests in protected areas
that are dark and warm,
like water meter boxes,
worm farms and upturned pots.

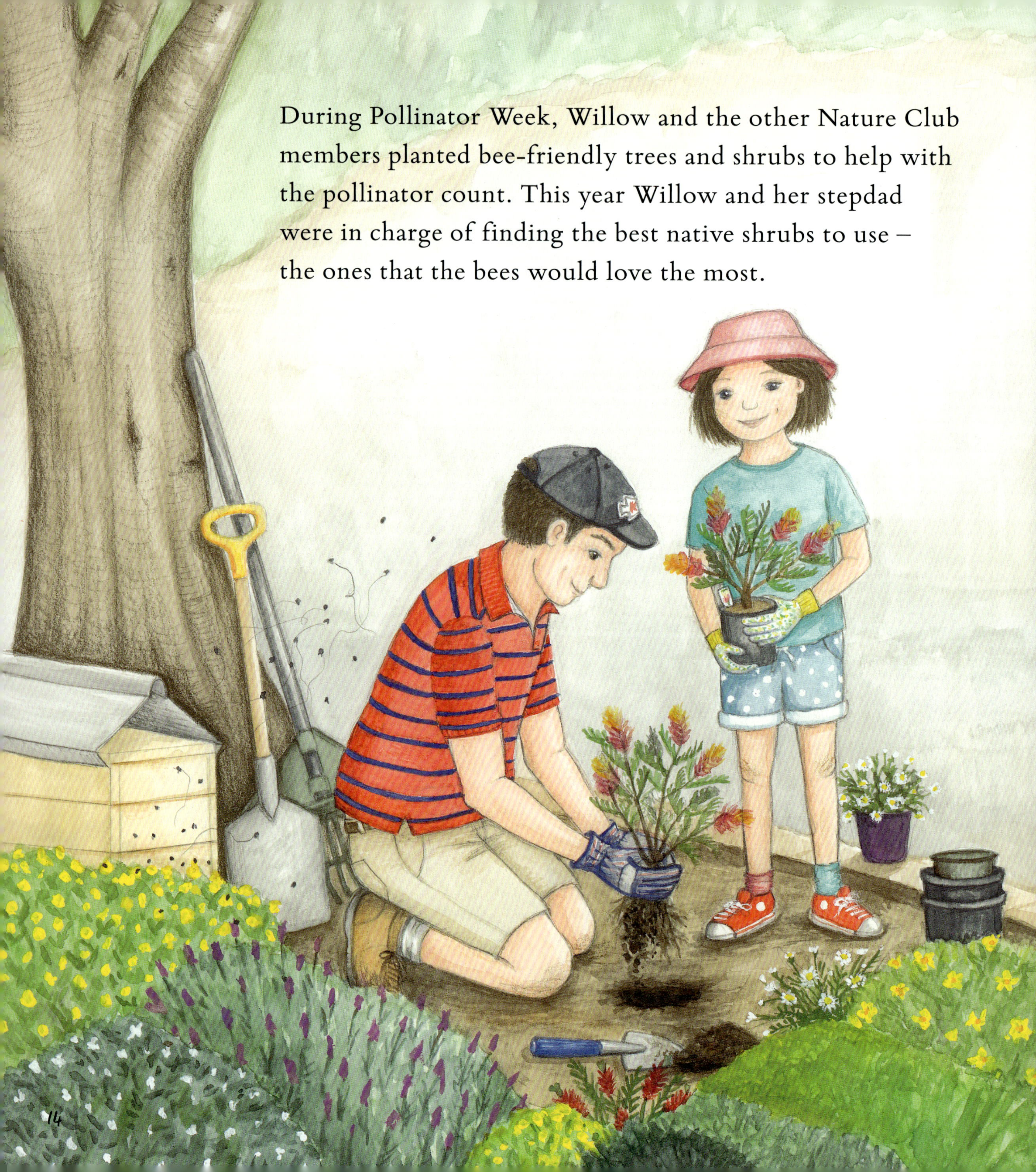

During Pollinator Week, Willow and the other Nature Club members planted bee-friendly trees and shrubs to help with the pollinator count. This year Willow and her stepdad were in charge of finding the best native shrubs to use – the ones that the bees would love the most.

Native bees are prolific pollinators and are vital for the pollination of flora in bushland and national parks, along with other pollinators including honey bees, bugs, beetles, ants, birds, bats and possums.

Native bees and honey bees are also crucial for pollination of crops which are an important part of the food we eat.

Hive day was here! But the air was hot and humid and Willow was anxious that it might be too hot to split the hive. Making a quick check, Willow noticed that the bees had arranged themselves around the entrance, fanning their wings to cool down.

Worker bees ventilate the hives by fanning their wings to draw cool air inside, and control the humidity in the hive by drinking the excess moisture and then spitting it out of the entrance of the nest. Overheating, extreme cold and natural disasters can be dangerous for bees.

When bees live in a man-made environment, the timber OATH (Original Australian Trigona Hive) box is often used as a home.

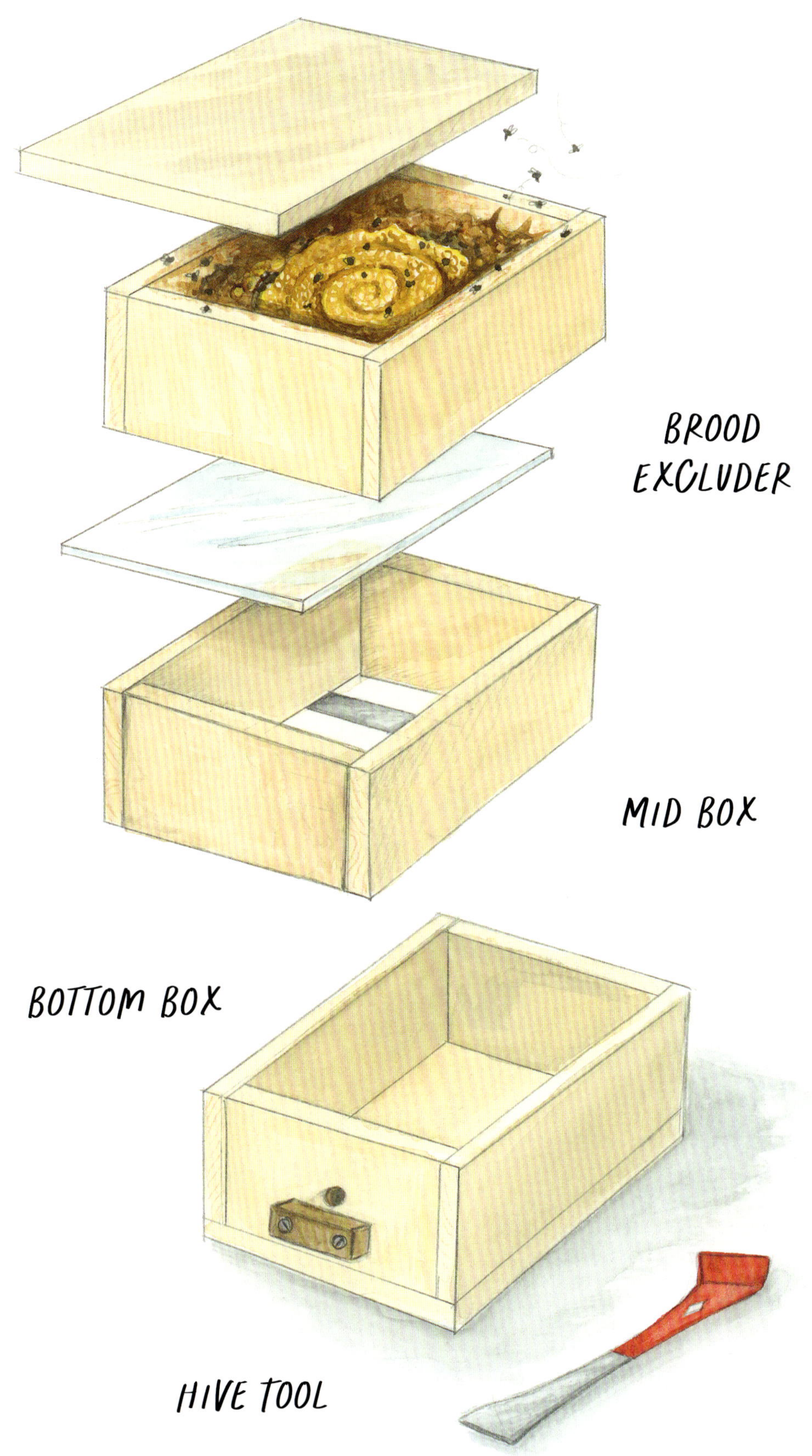

Willow relaxed when Tom announced that it was cool enough for the divide to begin!

Tom used his *hive tool* to separate the top and bottom sections of the parent hive, glued tightly with propolis. He spoke calmly to the bees and as the hive layers separated, the *brood nest* gently pulled apart showing thick and sticky multi-layered rings of the richest brown.

When a hive is divided, half will be without a queen. The queen bee is easy to spot and will be surrounded by a court of attending worker bees.

Bees hovered around Tom's beard and zipped about his face. He walked the circle of students with the bottom section of the hive, letting them gently push their fingers inside some of the honey pots surrounding the brood, while others peeled off excess propolis to smell its strong scent.

'Can I visit your hive one day?' asked Willow's friend. Willow smiled and nodded as she tickled bees off her hands and hair.

Native stingless bees build complex nests for protection. Native bees rear their young in **brood comb** and store food in honey pots and pollen pots made of resin, propolis and wax secreted from glands on the abdomens of bees.

The full top of the hive was placed gently on the empty bottom of Willow's new home hive box. The bottom of the school hive was returned to the stand and an empty top section was added and strapped together. The bees would soon glue the halves back to a whole with propolis.

Willow's box had the ventilation holes loosely plugged with fabric to keep the bees inside.

The divided hive will need to establish a new queen to survive. Once a queen is found, the new colony will settle and begin work. The male drones fertilise the queen, who lays the eggs, and the female worker bees do the majority of the work.

At home, Willow and her stepdad placed the hive under the canopy of the tea-tree plants. Her stepdad said that the sweet *nectar* would make the area 'like a lolly shop for bees'. Willow removed the fabric. As the bees began an *orientation flight* she chatted to them, introducing them to the chickens, the honey bees and the resident mottled-skinned blue-tongued lizard.

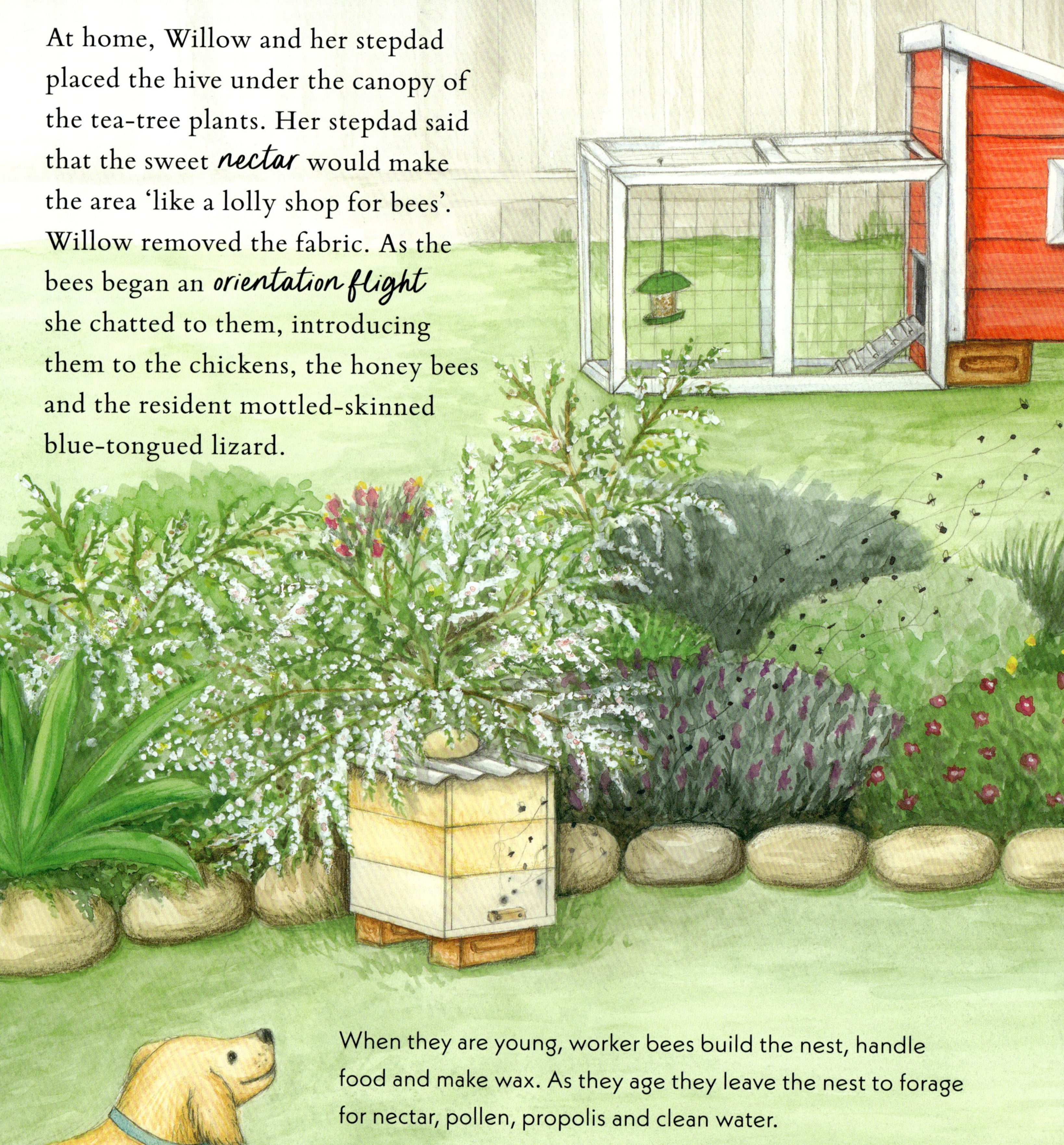

When they are young, worker bees build the nest, handle food and make wax. As they age they leave the nest to forage for nectar, pollen, propolis and clean water.

The new colony began the work of sorting their hive and foraging.

As the sun began to fade, Willow watched the gentle sparkle of bee wings streaming in through the hive entrance, everyone settled at last.

Native bees thrive when people establish bee-friendly gardens, avoid spraying with insecticides, and provide habitats for bees by using old timber logs or bee hotels.

Pollinator counts contribute to our knowledge of Australia's pollinating species and help count and record the diversity of insects.

INDEX

About the Author

Megan Daley is a multiple award-winning teacher librarian, author, speaker, podcaster, literary judge and loves wandering literature festivals. Megan's best subjects at high school were English and Agriculture and she still adores reading, writing, small-scale farming, growing green things, chickens and bees.

Megan lives in humid Brisbane where she waits for it to be cool enough to split her hives and lives with her partner, a commercial beekeeper, and their children, Ava, Georgia Willow, Sam and Jimmy.

About the Illustrator

Max Hamilton is an award-winning illustrator, graphic designer and, most enthusiastically, a maker of children's books. She enjoys noticing the little details in things, loves to get lost in the world of illustration and stories and, through her art, aims to raise awareness of the importance of protecting our Australian fauna.

Max lives in Sydney with her partner, two daughters, a fluffy dog and two guinea pigs named Dumpling and Noodles.

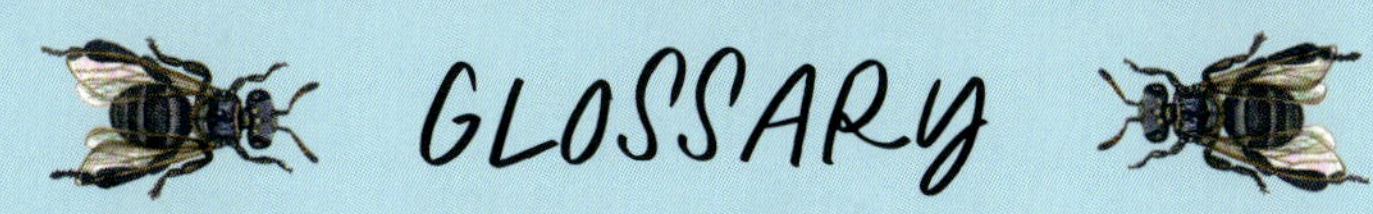

Beeswax: the soft wax produced by native bees in the glands near their abdomen.

Brood: the comb area of a nest where the queen bee lays eggs and worker bees raise the young.

Colony: a group of bees headed by a queen, working cooperatively to rear their young and sustain themselves.

Forage: locate and return valuable food and building resources to the colony.

Hive: the home (man-made or natural) of a colony of bees, their stored food and building materials.

Honey: a unique and complex food only produced by bees. Native bee honey is thinner and is often referred to as sugarbag honey.

Nectar: a sugar liquid normally found at the base of a flower and sucked up by bees using their straw-like tongue.

Orientation flight: bees become familiar with a new habitat by performing small manoeuvres in the air, going a little further on each flight.

Pollen: high protein food source for many insects and animals, particularly bees, ants, birds and bats.

Propolis: a mix of resin, wax and pollen.

Resin: a sticky substance produced by plants and collected by native stingless bees as they forage.

Look up the pages to find out about all these bee-related things.
Don't forget to look at both kinds of words – this kind and this kind.

For the best children's books, look for the bear.

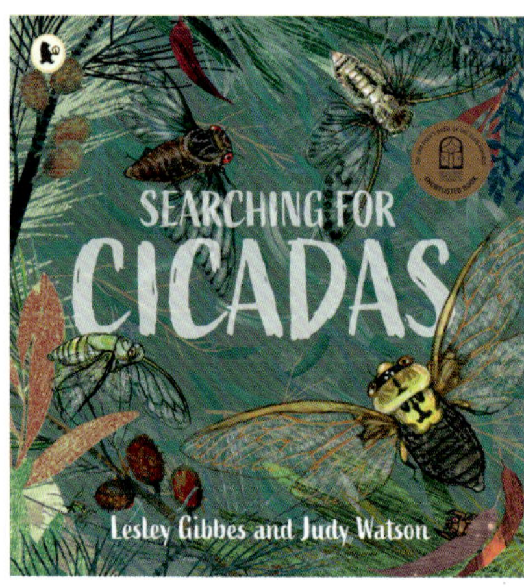

SEARCHING FOR CICADAS
by Lesley Gibbes
illustrated by Judy Watson

This picture book brings together award winners Lesley Gibbes and Judy Watson to showcase the wonder and beauty of cicadas as well as highlight the common summer pastime of cicada-watching.

In the summertime, Grandpa and I go cicada-watching. We put our camping gear into my wagon and walk down to the local reserve. Last year we saw five Green Grocers, three Yellow Mondays and one Floury Baker. Can we find the rare Black Prince this year?

SHORTLISTED, EVE POWNALL AWARD FOR INFORMATION BOOKS, CBCA BOOK OF THE YEAR AWARDS

"Readers will pore over the pages looking at the incredible detail … the detailed cicada will draw entreaties to go out and see them for themselves."
ReadPlus

Paperback ISBN: 978-1-760655-48-8

WEDGE–TAILED EAGLE
by Claire Saxby
illustrated by Christina Booth

Award-winning author Claire Saxby's latest addition to the Nature Storybook series, following a female wedge-tailed eagle and her mate in a lyrical, fact-filled look at Australia's largest raptor.

Look up. Way up, into the clear blue. Those two tiny specks are a wedge-tailed eagle and her mate.

The largest raptor in Australia, wedge-tailed eagles are powerful hunters who mate for life, bringing many new clutches of chicks into the world in their lifetime. Award-winning author Claire Saxby leads us through a mating season, while Christina Booth's illustrations capture the majesty, power and gentleness of these magnificent birds of prey.

"Another lesson on nature's miracles to add to this fabulous series!"
Kids' Book Review

Paperback ISBN: 978-1-761601-79-8

GREAT WHITE SHARK
by Claire Saxby
illustrated by Cindy Lane

The great white shark swims on.
Her tail sways side-to-side;
her fins keep her balanced.
She travels the fast lane
where she can, cruising
invisible seaways

In *Great White Shark* we follow a female shark on her way to warmer waters to give her pups the best chance of survival. Set in a stunning underwater world, Claire Saxby's signature poetic prose and Cindy Lane's sublime illustrations showcase the grace, majesty and power of one of the ocean's top predators.

WINNER, BEST CHILDREN'S BOOK, ROYAL ZOOLOGICAL SOCIETY OF NSW WHITLEY AWARD
SHORTLISTED, CBCA AWARD FOR NEW ILLUSTRATORS, CBCA BOOK OF THE YEAR AWARDS

"Stunning illustrations grace this account … A splashing success."
Kirkus Reviews

Paperback ISBN: 978-1-760653-89-7